THE GREEN MAN

Richard Hayman

SHIRE PUBLICATIONS

Published in Great Britain in 2011 by Shire Publications Ltd, Midland House, West Way, Botley, Oxford OX2 0PH, United Kingdom.

44-02 23rd Street, Suite 219, Long Island City, NY 11101

E-mail: shire@shirebooks.co.uk   www.shirebooks.co.uk

A CIP catalogue record for this book is available from the British Library.

Shire Library no. 593   •   ISBN-13: 978 0 74780 784 1

Richard Hayman has asserted his right under the Copyright, Designs and Patents Act, 1988, to be identified as the author of this book.

Designed by Tony Truscott Designs, Sussex, UK and typeset in Perpetua and Gill Sans.
Printed in China through Worldprint Ltd.

11 12 13 14 15   10 9 8 7 6 5 4 3 2

COVER IMAGE
Green men feature in bosses at the east end of Exeter Cathedral, as here in the Lady Chapel, completed by 1291. The foliage has been interpreted as silverweed or mugwort.

CONTENTS PAGE IMAGE
This head spewing hawthorn leaves is at the end, or respond, of an arcade at Sutton Benger (Wiltshire). The naturalistic portrayal is typical of the fourteenth century, although it was apparently 'improved' during John Hakewill's restoration of the church in 1849.

TITLE PAGE IMAGE
The choir stalls at Whalley (Lancashire), made in the 1420s for Whalley Abbey but moved to the parish church when the abbey was closed, incorporate green-man carvings on the canopies and misericords.

ACKNOWLEDGEMENTS
The images on page 11 are reproduced by permission of Bildarchiv Foto Marburg. The following images are reproduced by permission of the British Library Board: page 10, lower (Harley 2904, f4); page 11 (Harley 4772, f5); and page 13 (additional ms 14788, f6). Other photographs are by the author.

Shire Publications is supporting the Woodland Trust, the UK's leading woodland conservation charity, by funding the dedication of trees.

CONTENTS

ORIGINS
AND DEFINITIONS

A NYONE with even a passing interest in history has heard of green men.
They have become one of the most familiar images from medieval
church architecture and appear in various guises: faces with greenery issuing
from the mouth, nose or eyes; faces from which leaves appear to grow; and
human faces disguised as leaves. They were popular images in European
churches from the twelfth to the sixteenth centuries, until – like every other
kind of medieval image – they became unfashionable and faded from the
repertoire of applied art.

The term 'green man' does not have any currency earlier than the 1930s.
Although none of them are green, and only a proportion of them are men,
the name has stuck and the alternatives, 'foliate head', 'leaf mask' and 'leaf
head', have not caught on. That the term has become firmly established is
due initially to Lady Raglan, who was inspired to enquire into the green man
in the church at Llangwm Uchaf near her home at Cefntilla in
Monmouthshire. In 1939 she published an article in the journal of the
Folklore Society in which she argued that the green man in church
architecture was a relic of pagan nature worship that had somehow weathered
several centuries of Christian culture. It was a thesis that extended arguments
put forward by the anthropologist Sir James Frazer in his multi-volume study
of primal religion, *The Golden Bough* (1890–1915). The prevalence in some
parts of England of Green Man public houses suggested the name, although
the pub names derived from leaf-clad figures of folk custom rather than heads
from which leaves grow. Lady Raglan's studies coincided with a detailed
survey of roof bosses in English churches and cathedrals, in which many
green-man carvings were described for the first time. It encouraged the view
that these were 'pagan' images on the margin of a later culture, the work of
anonymous craftsmen stubbornly resisting orthodox Christian teaching and
carving green men as a silent affirmation of an older faith.

Throughout the 1950s and beyond, the idea of green man as pagan
survival was uncontroversial. It was assimilated into Nikolaus Pevsner's
Buildings of England architectural guides, while the literary critic John Speirs

Opposite:
The gurning faces
of the green men
in the porch at
Nantwich
(Cheshire) belong
to the restoration
of the church in
the 1850s by
Sir George Gilbert
Scott.

5

Right: The capitals on the chancel arch at Llangwm Uchaf (Monmouthshire) were carved in the fourteenth century. It was these carvings that inspired Lady Raglan to write the pioneering study in which she coined the term 'green man'.

Below: A detailed study of roof bosses was made in the 1930s and 1940s by C.J.P. Cave, who described many green-man carvings for the first time, like this example in the cloisters of Norwich Cathedral.

Above right: Exeter Cathedral has several classic green-man carvings of the late thirteenth century on the misericords and, as illustrated here, on roof bosses.

interpreted the fourteenth-century poem *Sir Gawain and the Green Knight* as a story about the green man. Upon this foundation the green man was reinterpreted in the latter part of the twentieth century to suit the needs of the post-modern world, as representing some sort of spiritual union with nature – but usually by concentrating on the green men and editing out the green masks, demons, dragons and feline heads of the medieval world.

Knowledge of churches, of the rise of Christianity and of pre-Christian religions has grown enormously over the past half century and the assumptions made about the green man in the 1950s are no longer convincing. We now know that the green man did not exist in Britain prior to Christianity, that the popularity of the image in western Europe is the product of Christianity, and that in England and Wales it fell out of favour and declined with the whole iconography of medieval art in the mid-sixteenth century.

Green-man carvings are prevalent enough to deserve a proper explanation, but have attracted very little interest from the academic world. Most of what we know has been the work of independent historians, but it has been easier to explore the origins of green-man carvings than to understand them.

Antecedents of the green man can be traced to classical antiquity, and a case has been made that the origin of the image is to be found in India, but this does not help us understand its meaning in the medieval world. Images are transferable across cultures but the meanings are much less stable. For example, many exotic creatures such as unicorns and elephants found their way into Christian iconography, mainly drawn from pagan classical authors, but they were reinterpreted according to Christian morality. Meanings have continued to change. The swastika was a common symbol in Buddhism, Jainism, Christianity and Hinduism but acquired new sinister connotations in the 1930s. The owl symbolises wisdom, but in the medieval

Crowcombe (Somerset) has one of the most rewarding sets of bench ends in an English church, carved in 1534. In this example, the best known, a mask is deliberately rendered ugly by its asymmetrical features; he has mermen emerging from his ears in addition to the vines spewing out of his mouth.

A green-man festival is held every year at Clun (Shropshire), in which the green man symbolises spring overcoming winter, but the meaning and rituals are a modern invention. This reinterpretation of the green man is a classic example of how meanings change over time.

7

In this supporting carving on a fourteenth-century misericord at Gayton (Northamptonshire), oak leaves and a crown are used as symbols of honour, just as garlands, laurels and palm branches had been in Biblical and classical times.

world it stood for ignorance, especially that of Jews who lived in the darkness and shunned the light of Christianity.

Faces disgorging leaves are sometimes found in Roman architecture. The face of Oceanus, a Roman sea god, is occasionally depicted as a head with hair and beard of seaweed. Two of the best surviving examples of the latter have been found in Britain – on a fourth-century silver plate at Mildenhall (Suffolk), now in the British Museum, and on a floor mosaic from Maiden Newton (Dorset). Leaf heads have been found associated with second- and third-century sarcophagi at Neumagen in the Rhineland, implying that they were associated with the afterlife – the job of Oceanus was to take the dead across the ocean to the land of Bacchus. But no direct descent can be traced from these images to medieval green men.

Uncertain origins are only one obstacle to understanding medieval green men. They are difficult to interpret because there is no literature that describes them, unlike almost every other image in medieval iconography. For example, we know that the dragon is an incarnation of the devil because the bestiaries (or books of beasts) tell us so. Without the help of literature we have to consider the broader context of the image. This chapter looks at the significance of trees and plants in Christian thought and art. The following chapters look at the kinds of faces and vegetation association with green men, the architectural context, specifically the potential significance of where green-man carvings are placed, and their relationship with other images.

Trees and plants are a meaningful presence in the Bible, in which they stand for much more than humanity's relationship with nature. There were two trees at the centre of the Garden of Eden – the Tree of Life and the Tree of the Knowledge of Good and Evil with its forbidden fruit. Greenery is often associated with supernatural events, as when God manifested himself to Moses by means of a burning bush on the 'mountain of God'. There is even a Biblical image very like the later green man. In the Old Testament, God points out to Ezekiel a group of idolaters and says, 'look at them putting the branch to their nose', but it is unlikely that such an obscure reference to idolatrous practice is the precise meaning of the medieval green man.

In John's Gospel, Christ described himself as 'the true vine' and in the parable of the mustard seed Jesus describes how the seed will grow into a great tree in which all the birds of the air find shelter. Good and evil are therefore both associated with trees in different ways.

When Christ entered Jerusalem, his path was strewn with palm branches, an ancient symbol of respect that was not confined to Christianity or Judaism. Branches are associated with kingship in such different cultures as pagan Ireland and the Hebrew Bible, as if the branch symbolised the king's special relationship with the forces of Nature and the supernatural world, which authenticated his rule. Virgil's epic first-century poem, *The Aeneid*, also reminds us of the ancient use of garlands as a mark of esteem, in this case conferred upon winners of sporting contests. In the Bible, Christ is mocked by Roman soldiers who place a crown of thorns on his head. The honorific use of garlands and laurels remained familiar in the Middle Ages. The 'hallowing of fronds' was one of the earliest established parish customs, in which the priests blessed branches that were carried in processions on Palm Sunday, remembering Christ's triumphant entry into Jerusalem.

The idea of trees as a wider symbol of natural growth has been current since the work of Herodotus, writing in the fifth century BC, in which the mother of the Persian emperor Cyrus has a dream that branches grow out

This capital on the twelfth-century crossing arch at Melbourne (Derbyshire) shows a demon, his legs splayed to reveal his testicles, biting a branch, which he has bent over. It symbolises the work of the Devil, deforming but not quite destroying the work of God.

The wild man is shown on a fifteenth-century misericord at Whalley, next to a woman, in order to contrast savagery with civilisation. Wild men personify wild nature but they are not green men.

from between her legs. It was a sign that her son would found a dynasty that would rule the known world. In Christian art the image of growth was used to portray the genealogy of Christ and his ancestor David, which was especially popular in stained glass. It is known as a Tree of Jesse, named after the father of David, from whose loins a tree grows.

Christianity's attitude to nature is as ambivalent and complicated as any other culture. Nature was a moral entity because everything in Creation had a purpose, which enabled the sinner to see the world of humankind reflected in the world of plants and animals. Hildegard of Bingen, the twelfth-century abbess and mystic, remarked that, before the Flood, the world was a place of gentle rivers and pleasant woods, but God had transformed them into torrents and impenetrable forests. Greenery could be associated with good and evil, but it usually had the latter association in medieval art. An influential ninth-century theologian, Rabanus Maurus, described leaves as representing lust and the sins of the flesh. Forests in medieval Europe were places of beauty but also places of danger where the devil lurked. In the life of St Ailred it is claimed that the monks established an abbey at Rievaulx (North Yorkshire) in

Below right: This Psalter, or psalm book, produced in England in the tenth century, is one of the earliest examples in book illustration of a demon sprouting foliage, here as an integral part of the ornamented letter B.

Opposite: In these creation scenes from a Bible produced in Languedoc, southern France, devilish masks are used at the margins as a decorative feature, sprouting the foliage around the edges of the picture.

a secluded valley that was like a 'second paradise of wooded delight'. By contrast a fourteenth-century friar, Bartholomaeus Anglicus, described such forests as places where robbers lurk, and where treacherous men confused would-be travellers by false signs, all of which are allegories of the way that the devil lured the faithful from the path of righteousness.

The forests of Europe were the medieval equivalent of the Biblical desert. Here could be found a mythical personification of wild nature, the Wild Man (also known as a Woodhouse or Woodwose). Wild men lived beyond the bounds of civilisation, devilish creatures incapable of reason and ruled by animal instinct. Another type of wild man, familiar from medieval tales such as *Yvain*, was the social outcast living like a wild animal, enduring the torments of the wilderness that punish and purify him, which would eventually lead to his salvation. Both types are present in medieval art but they are not green men.

Green men first appear in medieval art in book illustrations from the tenth century, especially in France, and grew in popularity in the eleventh and twelfth centuries. During this period there was a significant growth in the number of monasteries, and hence also the need for books and the training of scribes capable of producing them. These books included Bibles, books of Psalms (Psalters), Homilies and the works of the leading theologians of the Roman Catholic church, known as the Four Doctors. Of these, Gregory's *Moralia in Job*, a commentary on the Old Testament Book of Job, was especially popular. In book illustrations, green men are never the main subject, but appear in the borders framing larger pictures, or as part of the pictorial flourishes used to adorn the initial letters of chapters. They sprout profuse tangled branches that betray their origin in the

The initial M is clearly a demon sprouting, or possibly biting, long stems of stylised plants, and has aggressive serpents emerging from his ears. It comes from a twelfth-century German Passional – a book describing the sufferings of martyrs and saints.

interlace ornament of Saxon and Celtic art. They have an obvious stylistic practicality in terminating decorative foliage trails in the same manner that serpents bite their own or other serpents' tails in the art of the same period. Tanglewood was also a metaphor for the human condition, since what trapped men physically also impeded them spiritually. Few of these so-called

This dedication page was made in the eleventh century for a manuscript volume, or codex, which was originally presented to Archbishop Egbert of Trier, c. 980. The margins are decorated with stylised plants emerging from the mouths of demon masks.

A page from a
Bible produced in
Belgium in the
mid-twelfth
century shows
tanglewood issuing
from the mouths
of monsters, filling
the background.

green men are actually men. They are devils' heads, human masks or cats' heads. Cats were creatures of the night and were therefore associated with the devil, which might serve to link all foliage-sprouting creatures with evil, except that not all of them were meant so seriously. Foliage sprouts from the mouths of a diverse range of creatures from acrobats to fish, images that take a typical medieval delight in the absurd.

Images in books were an important source of inspiration for the patrons of churches, and it seems that this was the direct source from which green men first appeared in churches.

ROMANESQUE CHURCHES

CARVINGS of green men first appear in churches in the eleventh and twelfth centuries. Their emergence was not an isolated event but part of a new vocabulary of art and architecture that came with a surge in church building after the millennium. In 1125 William of Malmesbury described Westminster Abbey as built in a 'style that now all seek to emulate at vast expense'. The style is termed 'Romanesque' because it took Roman architecture as its model, and it spanned the eleventh and twelfth centuries. Most English Romanesque churches belong to the period after the Norman Conquest, for which reason the style is generally known in England as Norman. It was a great period of Christian enthusiasm, when cathedrals were rebuilt and new monasteries were founded. At a local level it was the final stage in the evolution of the parish system and a period when many parish churches were rebuilt in stone.

With these new buildings came a new language of ornament. Romanesque architecture was richly decorated. Its carved scenes or figures were mainly applied to key focal points such as doorway and window surrounds and the chancel arch, which separated the nave (the secular part of the church) from the chancel (the sacred part of the church occupied by the priests). Other important symbolic focal points that were richly decorated included fonts, baptism being one of the most important rites of passage in Christian life. The subject matter of architectural carving was primarily religious, although not exclusively so. In some cases it is difficult to establish a definite religious theme, although they can often be inferred. For example, the carving of a tree is usually interpreted as the Tree of Life described in Genesis and Revelation. Of images representing sin and the forces of evil, demons and monsters are the most obvious examples. Green men were part of this new repertoire of architectural ornament, and the idea of applying them to buildings seems to have been imported from northern France, the single most important outside influence on English architecture. Another image imported from France at the same time was the well known 'sheila-na-gig', or lustful woman, who had a similar connotation to the green man as a fellow sinner.

Opposite: Leominster Priory (Herefordshire) was re-founded in 1123 and has richly decorated Norman work. It includes green men on the capitals of the internal arches of its west doorway. On one side the face is a smooth mask, and on the other it has a tortured expression.

Lullington (Somerset) was a manor owned by King Harold, which William the Conqueror gave to his compatriot the Bishop of Coutances after 1066. Its Romanesque carvings include this green man on one of the tower-arch capitals.

Churches in the eleventh and twelfth centuries were built by wealthy patrons, rather than the parish communities who were responsible for many parish churches in the later Middle Ages. Many of our parish churches began life as the private estate chapels of local lords. The small scale of many of these churches should not be taken as a sign that they were humble buildings, because the reverse was often the case. Not only were these churches built by wealthy patrons, it was sometimes the patrons themselves who suggested decorative schemes. Freemasons did not enjoy a free hand in carved ornamentation but were directed by patrons and

Linley (Shropshire) was a private estate chapel of the Linley family, built in the twelfth century. It has north and south doorways. This, the north, was probably the most important as it has the richest treatment. There is a full-length figure with oversized head, and thus probably a demon, sprouting branches.

Several of the capitals at Northampton St Peter show masks emitting foliage that are derived from manuscript illuminations. On this capital the heads are like a chain, a device also found on a font at Holt (Worcestershire).

This twelfth-century grave slab at Northampton St Peter, possibly from a shrine to St Ragener, has a bearded head emitting stylised branches while a bird pecks at his ear. The curved branches frame a dragon, serpent and a dog biting a goat.

clergymen who either suggested a model from which they could copy, or introduced ideas from illuminated manuscripts. Green men appeared in churches because they were part of the developing tastes of the people who paid for the churches to be built.

Two examples of elite patronage – Northampton St Peter and Kilpeck (Herefordshire) – demonstrate well how green-man carvings emerged in British churches. Northampton St Peter was built in the 1140s by Simon de St Lys in the precinct of his castle, and was probably a private chapel rather than a parish church. The plan of the original church copied the Roman basilica form, which meant that it has arcades that separate nave and aisles. The church is distinguished by its lavish decoration, demonstrating the wealth and sophistication of its patron. The capitals feature many designs of stylised foliage, and several of them incorporate foliage emerging from the mouths of masks. Sources of the many motifs inside and outside the church have been traced to English manuscript illuminations, in particular English Psalters of the mid-twelfth century and a copy of Gregory's *Moralia*. It is possible that someone like Simon de St Lys owned or had access to similar books.

Kilpeck has a small church that stands next to a motte-and-bailey castle, built by Hugh of Kilpeck and completed by 1134. At the east end it has a vaulted semi-circular apse that copies the tomb of St Peter at Rome, a feature found at some other contemporary churches in England. It is also one of the first

17

Above: The green man on the doorway at Kilpeck (Herefordshire) is a primitive mask, quite different from the human heads carved inside the church. He is disgorging a stylised form of vine.

Right: The font at Stottesdon (Shropshire) is the work of the Herefordshire school of Romanesque carvers. It uses masks, which give the impression of sprouting branches, to link the medallions around the bowl.

churches in England to feature architectural sculpture, in the form of the superimposed apostles on the chancel arch, the inspiration for which came from western France. This is significant because it suggests that Hugh of Kilpeck had passed through western France on a pilgrimage to Santiago de Compostela in Spain, as other contemporary Herefordshire barons had done. Among Kilpeck's architectural carvings are creatures derived from the bestiaries that described fabulous and real creatures in terms of their moral attributes. Kilpeck is one of the first English churches in which bestiary creatures are represented, suggesting that its patron either owned or had seen one of these valuable books. Kilpeck therefore is a small church whose patron was at the cutting edge of artistic taste.

Kilpeck church also has green-man carvings. Two are on the capitals of the west window and the other is on one of the capitals of the south doorway. On the doorway a mask sprouting foliage is one of a complex series of images on the struggle between good and evil. One shaft depicts superimposed figures of knights entangled in foliage. The tanglewood represents the snares of the devil, ready to entrap the unwary that stray from the straight and narrow path of virtue. In the tympanum, which is the semi-circular panel above the doorway, is the Tree of Life.

Kilpeck is also typical in that the green men are not men but masks. The masks are deliberately quite different from the other human faces on the south doorway, and figures of apostles inside the church. The mask is a characterless stereotype. Human masks with foliage are commonly incorporated into larger decorative schemes surrounding doorways and chancel arches. Sometimes a meaning can be inferred, while at other times the green men / masks are probably decorative. Masks emitting, or perhaps even biting, foliage are also used as decorative devices on three closely related Shropshire fonts at Linley, Morville and Stottesdon, as well as the font at Brecon Cathedral. Here the mask is a convenient way of linking the medallions that decorate the font bowl. A similar repetitive device is used to frame the doorway at Charney Bassett (Oxfordshire).

On the ambitious Norman font at Shernborne (Norfolk), masks lurk on the underside of the bowl, emitting leafless stems.

The outer order of the doorway at Charney Bassett (Oxfordshire) is a frieze of heads sprouting leaves, or forked tongues, which amounted to much the same thing.

The tympanum at Elkstone (Gloucestershire) shows a simplified version of the Day of Judgement. Christ in the centre passes judgement, surrounded by symbols of the Four Evangelists. An angel on the left stands for those sent to heaven, a green man on the right represents the damned sent to hell.

19

The twelfth-century font at Bridekirk incorporates foliage in all its four faces. A double-headed beast [below] has foliage issuing from one of its mouths, while the other bites its own tail, which turns into a stem with leaves. On another face [right] are two dragons biting leaves, and a vine trail that emerges from the mouth of a demon mask, and is terminated by a man biting it. The overall theme is that baptism cleanses sins.

Several examples point to an association between green men and the devil. Elkstone (Gloucestershire) is one of the easier carvings to interpret. Its tympanum is a representation of the Day of Judgement, a common subject in medieval Christian art with a well-understood structure. The green man is on the side of the damned. Green men often appear on fonts, a place where evil is driven out and where all manner of evil creatures are portrayed. Bridekirk (Cumbria) has a twelfth-century font, the carvings on all four sides of which link virtue and sin with greenery. One shows two swordsmen

fighting over a woman who is either hugging or is tied to a tree. On the other sides, a Greek cross sprouts flowers; a double-headed monster sprouts foliage from one of its mouths while its tail turns into a stem with leaves; and monsters bite the leaves of

The twelfth-century font at Lullington (Somerset) has an upper band of feline heads issuing foliage, although it does not continue around the whole circumference of the bowl.

a plant above a foliage trail that issues from the mask of a demon and terminates with a man biting the fruit. The sequence concludes with the baptism of Christ, with a tree to the side.

Not all of these heads or masks are human. As in manuscript illuminations, a significant number are demons, monsters or animals. The most common animal is the cat or lion. The cats' devilish pointed ears further insinuate them with evil. Lullington (Somerset) font incorporates cats spewing foliage in the carvings around the rim, which is also accompanied by the Latin inscription translated as 'In this holy font sins perish and are washed away'. Elsewhere the animal is probably a lion, as on the doorway at Barton-le-Street (North Yorkshire) or the chancel arch at Castor (Cambridgeshire).

Luppitt (Devon) font has wild and vivid carvings on the general theme of sin, including a centaur fighting dragons, two men driving a stake into a man's head and this large satanic mask with foliage issuing from below its teeth.

Right: The head on the chancel arch at Garway (Herefordshire) is either a cat with pointed ears, or a devil with horns

Below: The tympanum at Llanbadarn Fawr (Powys) was set up in a Victorian church, and is placed within an arch slightly too large for it. Unusually it has a cat with a tree trunk sprouting from its head, with monsters attacking it, probably representing the Tree of the Knowledge of Good and Evil, with the demon as the root of all evil.

Lions and lionesses are associated with various virtues, but also with human weaknesses, although it is difficult to know precisely how such images would have been read by a medieval audience. Many are difficult to identify because they are simply stylised feline heads, pointed ears being their chief characteristic.

Foliage in Romanesque carving is stylised rather than natural, but was often modelled on the vine, if only because that was what was copied from books. Whether there is significance in the use of vines in green-man carvings

The twelfth-century tympanum at Dumbleton (Gloucestershire) is heavily restored, with a crude green man re-cut in the nineteenth century.

is debatable. It has been argued that faces issuing vines represent men breathing new life in heaven. Despite the obvious association between foliage and rebirth, and Christ's characterisation as the true vine, it is difficult to reconcile either concept with the vines issuing from the ugly mask at Kilpeck. Vines could have been just a general representation of foliage in a country where few carvers would have been familiar with them.

Above: A face spewing stylised foliage, like a forked tongue, is on the capital of the doorway at Longdon (Staffordshire).

Left: On the tympanum of the south doorway at Fritwell (Oxfordshire) two beasts roar at a tree, their tongues turning into branches with leaves.

GOTHIC ARCHITECTURE

A RCHITECTURE changed at the end of the twelfth century. The pointed arch superseded the round arch and, with the use of pointed rib vaults, new Gothic buildings were much stronger than older Romanesque buildings and could be built to increasing heights. A new approach to ornamentation came with it, one that was more linear than Romanesque and was dictated by the structural forms with which it was associated. Inevitably, therefore, the vocabulary of ornament changed and green men and other figure carvings became less popular, if only for a short time. In Gothic buildings green men appear regularly but not in the places they were in Norman churches. Doorways and the chancel arches were not so lavishly embellished as in Norman churches, and green men are less commonly found there.

Style was still dictated by a cultural elite of patrons and churchmen. The organisation of the medieval building trade meant that the design and supervision of a building was left to master masons. In the largest building projects they employed 'hewers' and rough masons to shape stone and lay it in courses, but the finer skills of carving and the erection of arches and vaults were left to skilled freemasons and setters. Green men in Gothic architecture were either designed by the master masons, or were the creation of freemasons who were working on a general theme. The other key skilled person in medieval building was the master carpenter, leader of a team that was engaged in structural work, but also in making smaller fixtures such as screens and choir stalls. Even in lesser churches, where there was a smaller hierarchy, the building was under the overall supervision of a master mason and carving was undertaken by freemasons, generally following the styles created in the larger churches.

Green men are found in Gothic churches in two main places: on the capitals of arches, and as bosses, the square or round decoration used to hide the junction of main roof timbers or ribs of stone vaults. Exceptions to this rule are numerous, especially in larger churches such as Southwell Minster (Nottinghamshire), which is described below. Very often the green man is carved on the capitals of arcade arches, at a time when churches were

Opposite:
Southwell Minster
(Nottinghamshire)
chapter house was
built in the late
thirteenth century.
In the gables above
the seats are
foliage carvings,
including this
green man and the
one on page 29,
disgorging
buttercups and
hops.

enlarged by the addition of aisles. The classic position for these, and generally speaking the place to find enriched carvings, is on the responds, which are the half-piers bonded into the wall at the ends of the arcades. At Sutton Benger (Wiltshire) one of the most exuberant of these carvings is found in just such a position. They are also found here on late-fifteenth-century arcades at Halse (Somerset), which are notable for their crudeness in comparison with a roundel of around 1300 that is re-set on the wall above.

Green men are not randomly dispersed on roofs. Roofs were carefully constructed so that green men often appear on the margins of the main subject matter. Two examples, Tewkesbury Abbey and Worcester Cathedral, reveal how green men colonise the minor spaces. In both of these churches there are vaults in nave and chancel, which have bosses that depict

important religious themes. At Worcester the green men are found in the cloisters, especially in the east walk leading from the main church to the chapter house. At Tewkesbury the green-man bosses are found in the aisles and the ambulatory, a processional way behind the altar. Norwich and Canterbury Cathedrals both have numerous green-man carvings, but again they are found in the cloisters rather than in the main body of the church. At Southwell

Above: This roundel, c. 1300, is at Halse (Somerset). It was probably not made for this church, but was set into the wall as a valuable piece of architectural salvage, probably after the Reformation. It is set in a wall above a late-medieval arcade in which there are green men of far inferior quality on the capitals.

Centre: The church at Ottery St Mary (Devon) was begun in 1337 for Bishop Grandison of Exeter, which accounts for its lavish architectural treatment, including several green-man carvings.

Right: These triple green men are on a capital of the tower arch at Belgrave (Leicestershire), a fourteenth-century embellishment of a late-twelfth-century arch.

Minster the chancel and the screen (or 'pulpitum') across the chancel are richly decorated with heads and foliage, but not with green men, who are confined to the relatively less important chapter house.

Green men lost some of their specific meaning from the Romanesque. Rather like dragons and other bestiary creatures that had moral connotations, they became a general image of sin but are used so widely, and not always in a structured fashion, that their impact is reduced. In some cases the association with sinfulness is clear. In Exeter Cathedral the chancel arcades have figures at the base of the wall shafts rising to the vaults, one of which shows the Virgin and Child

The cloister vaults at Worcester Cathedral feature green-man bosses only in the east walk, built in the 1380s, leading to the chapter house.

At Norwich Cathedral green-man bosses are to be found in the cloisters, built piecemeal from the early fourteenth to the early fifteenth century, rather than in the main body of the church.

In the late-thirteenth-century chancel at Exeter Cathedral are figure carvings at the base of the vault shafts. Here the Virgin Mary and Child are depicted with angels around their heads and trample evil underfoot, represented by a green man.

with angels around their heads and the devil – the green man – trampled underfoot.

The nature and style of green-man carvings changed during the Gothic era. Previously green men had been masks or feline heads sprouting foliage, but now another form became popular, the leaf head. Drawings of such figures were made by the Frenchman Villard de Honnecourt in the 1230s. In these the head does not sprout foliage but is composed of foliage, as if a pile of leaves is a human face in disguise. The devil was the ultimate master of disguise but not all of these leaf heads seem unequivocally evil. The style of carving also changed in the fourteenth century. Masks became unfashionable and the heads were much more like human faces. Similarly, stylised foliage went out of fashion and carvers produced naturalistic foliage. In both cases the green-man carvings simply follow the contemporary fashion for naturalism over stylised images.

Below left: There are many green-man capitals in the arches at Much Marcle (Herefordshire) that illustrate the naturalistic style of the fourteenth century. This man wears a cross-shaped brooch.

Below right: The chancel arch capital at Finedon (Northamptonshire) has naturalistic foliage typical of the fourteenth century, pulling a man's lips apart.

Naturalistic foliage is one of the hallmarks of the late thirteenth and early fourteenth centuries. At Pershore Abbey (Worcestershire) foliage is used on the bosses covering the junctions of the ribs in the chancel vault. Here, although the intention seems to have been to employ foliage bosses throughout, it

appears that the freemasons varied it slightly on three of the bosses, in which the foliage sprouts from human heads.

The building that perhaps best represents the naturalistic aspirations of the later thirteenth and fourteenth centuries is the chapter house at Southwell Minster. It shows that freemasons drew their inspiration from life and carved leaves that were well known to them, rather than the vines of earlier (and later) green men, with which most carvers had no direct experience.

The chapter house was built in the late thirteenth century, and has thirty-six seats, above which are gables filled with foliage, of which six contain green men. Maple, oak and hawthorn are the most popular leaf forms, but there are also hops, ivy and buttercups and, in two cases, birds to peck at the fruit. In one case a young man's face can be seen peering out between the branches, and is not actually disgorging vegetation. He could be a robber lying in wait, or perhaps his innocent face suggests a boy playing. The choice of leaves appears to have no magical or religious significance other than that they were common species that carvers knew well.

Until the late Middle Ages most green men were found in churches of high status such as cathedral, abbey or collegiate churches. The great cathedrals and the largest monasteries had been built by the end of the fourteenth century, with the exception of ancillary structures like cloisters. But the great era of parish church building was yet to come. It was not until the fifteenth and sixteenth centuries that green men appeared in parish churches in great numbers. As we saw in the twelfth century, parish churches were built by wealthy patrons, and the social elite continued to have a major role in patronising church architecture through the Middle Ages. There was a divided responsibility for the fabric of the parish church. The patrons of the church, usually a monastery, cathedral or local lord, were responsible for appointing parish priests and for providing the sacred part of the church building, the chancel. The parish was responsible for the remainder of the building. In the prosperous later Middle Ages large sums were spent on improving parish churches in what has been described as a golden age of church architecture. In many cases the whole parish was able to contribute something towards a parish building fund, perhaps by making donations, or organising fundraising events such as church ales.

Southwell Minster chapter house (Nottinghamshire) was built in the late thirteenth century. In the gable above this seat the green man attracts the attention of two birds and a fledgling. The leaves are ivy.

Above: The chancel roof at Spreyton (Devon) was built in 1451, largely at the instigation of the vicar. One of its roof bosses shows a human face disgorging foliage from the mouth and eye sockets, symbolising the decay of the flesh.

Left: The sixteenth-century roofs at South Tawton (Devon) have bosses of several masks or cadavers sprouting foliage.

Right: There are several green-man carvings on the late-medieval roofs at Sampford Courtenay (Devon), the most lifelike of which is this bearded man. He has more than a passing resemblance to Christ, but he is probably just another reminder that flesh is mortal.

Right: On the cornice of the chancel roof at Sampford Courtenay (Devon) this dragon's tail grows into a vine, which the dragon bites into at the other end, thus devouring itself.

Many fine wooden roofs were built in the fifteenth and sixteenth centuries, which are a wonderful heritage in their own right, and for decoration there were regional preferences. Look up at an East Anglian roof and you are likely to see a host of angels; in Leicestershire it will be a gallery of heads; but do the same thing in Devon and you are likely to see all manner of foliage bosses and many green men. Green men were usually carved on bosses, but occasionally appear on the cornices. There is less discernible structure to the placing of green men in parish church roofs than the larger churches.

This large roof boss in the north aisle at Queen Camel (Somerset) shows how, from the fifteenth century, there was a move away from naturalism and back to demon masks sprouting foliage, made more hideous here by showing its ugly teeth.

The chancel roof at Eaton-under-Heywood (Shropshire) was made c. 1500. Its bosses include grotesque figures and this ugly square mask issuing foliage.

Green-man bosses can be expected wherever there are large numbers of foliage bosses. In these late-medieval examples there was a shift to more stylised heads and foliage, and there was a return to the association between green men and sin and mortality. In Devon, cadaverous heads sprout foliage from the mouth and eye sockets, a reminder that flesh is mortal. In other cases they are hideous masks of flat faces, sometimes bearing their teeth, a type that is also found on bench ends and is described again later. There are good examples of naturalistic foliage, but in other cases the foliage is stylised, partly because they had to fit into a square shape to make a boss, and thus were subordinated to the structural form.

CHURCH FURNISHINGS

MEDIEVAL CHRISTIANITY was a highly visual culture and church interiors were decorated with a variety of imagery on the walls and in the windows. In addition, imagery was applied to church furnishings, the quantity and range of which increased throughout the Middle Ages. The most prevalent images in churches were of Biblical scenes, especially the crucifixion, and of saints, although most of them were destroyed during the Reformation of the mid-sixteenth century. Green men are found on many types of furnishing although, because they were not a target of iconoclastic religious reformers in the sixteenth and seventeenth centuries, they have gained a higher profile among the applied arts of the Middle Ages than they had at the time.

Romanesque fonts were often decorated with masks or monsters disgorging foliage, but the fashion for them declined in the thirteenth century. As Gothic style was more linear, and derived most of its ornamentation from foliage, figure sculpture does not appear on fonts very regularly from the thirteenth century onwards. Fourteenth- and fifteenth-century fonts featuring green-man carvings, such as those of Leckhampstead (Buckinghamshire) and Lostwithiel (Cornwall), are notable because they are infrequent. Green men appear rarely in stained glass, where saints and Biblical scenes predominated; and they do not feature in wall painting.

Most green men in church furnishing were carved out of wood, and they can be found on choir stalls, misericords, bench ends and occasionally on screens. Carpenters who worked on the roofs of buildings also engaged in making furnishings, but there is little evidence that the same carvers were responsible for, say, roofs and benches in a single church, because the two were rarely built at the same time. Pulpits did not appear in large numbers in churches until the fifteenth and sixteenth centuries and are not places on which green men are expected to appear. Likewise green men are uncommon on rood screens. Rood screens stood between the nave and chancel and were a structured composition in which much of the Christian message could be read. Saints were at the lowest level, and above the screen

Opposite:
Two green-man bench ends at Cothelstone (Somerset) are among several examples in the Quantock Hills where the green man is a hideous flat-faced mask with a protruding tongue and, often, bearing its teeth.

Green-man carvings sometimes appear on screens, as here at Strensham (Worcestershire), in what was probably originally a rood screen but was later moved to the west end of the church.

was the crucified Christ with the Virgin Mary and John the Baptist beside him. The wall above displayed the Day of Judgement, or Doom, painting, and a starry firmament, perhaps with angels, was painted onto the ceiling above it. Green men do, however, appear in a small number of rood screens in the border counties of England and Wales. In some of these, green men appear on the long foliage friezes that decorate the cornices of the screens, and can be interpreted either as disgorging or biting the foliage trail. They are reminiscent of the beasts biting their own tails in Saxon and Celtic art, and can be interpreted as being among the snares and impediments of earthly life.

Choir stalls were the earliest form of seating found in churches. Their seats are hinged so that when they are tipped up they reveal a ledge supported by a bracket, known as a misericord. In the Middle Ages monks and secular canons spent long hours standing in the choir stalls, singing the various daily offices of regular worship. As a concession, initially to the tired limbs of older monks, the ledge was provided for them to lean against while giving the impression of standing. Misericords were found only in cathedral, monastic and

Llananno (Powys) is a Victorian church but has the best-surviving piece of work by the medieval mid-Wales school of woodcarvers. On its rood screen is a dragon disgorging, or perhaps biting, a vine trail.

Pennant Melangell (Powys) is another work of the mid-Wales school and the vine trail on the rood screen issues from a skull or demon, returning to the theme of sin and mortality.

Misericords include many animal or demon faces sprouting foliage, as with this late-fourteenth-century ape from Hereford All Saints.

Misericords at Kings Lynn St Margaret (Norfolk) were made in the 1370s. The naturalistic treatment of the face, from the mouth of which grow oversized oak leaves, is typical of the period.

A fifteenth-century misericord at Great Doddington (Northamptonshire) shows the late-medieval reversion to stylised faces and vines in green-man carvings.

This mid-fifteenth century misericord at Cartmel Priory (Cumbria) shows a tricephalos, or three-headed Beelzebub. The outer faces disgorge leaves.

collegiate churches where the priests were required to sing this daily order of services. Very often a college was founded as part of a parish church, and so misericords were sometimes found in parish churches as well as abbeys and cathedrals. Many choir stalls and misericords were also salvaged for use in parish churches after the monasteries were dissolved in the 1530s.

Wood carvers found the undersides of misericords impossible to resist. The earliest surviving set of carved misericords is at Salisbury Cathedral, completed in the 1230s. The misericords are essentially foliage, but in many examples branches or stems emanate from a small head at the base of the carving. It was an aesthetically pleasing way of finishing the design, and one in which the diminutive green men play a supporting role. When a full range of subject matter was developed for misericords, green men became part of the repertoire. At Exeter Cathedral the misericords were produced between 1240 and 1270 and it is the earliest set with figure carvings. Three of them are masks with foliage growing from the head.

Misericords have been likened to the margins of medieval manuscripts, where witty asides were made to counterbalance the main subject matter. Green men, like scatological humour, grotesque faces, the battle of the sexes and bestiary monsters, are found at their best on misericords. Style followed the fashions seen in stone carving. So in the fourteenth century human faces and naturalistic foliage were common, like the well-known example at King's Lynn St Margaret (Norfolk), but in the later fifteenth and sixteenth centuries there was a reversion to masks and stylised foliage. Great Doddington's (Northamptonshire) green man is a nondescript face spewing out stylised

The misericords at Whalley (Lancashire) include a tricephalos that was probably the model for the similar misericord at Cartmel Priory.

Choir stalls at St David's Cathedral (Pembrokeshire) were made in the final decade of the fifteenth century and the first decade of the sixteenth, and include this conventional green man.

vines, quite different from its near neighbour, a wood carver at his work bench, who is portrayed in a more naturalistic style. Whalley (Lancashire) and Cartmel Priory (Cumbria) have fifteenth-century green men as three-headed devils.

Choir stalls were a major work in their own right. Some of them even include green men, like the modest heads on the restored screen at Whalley (Lancashire) or the aggressive figures above the stalls at Winchester Cathedral that vomit their foliage. The latter were carved in the early fourteenth century under the direction of William Lyngwode, a master carpenter who also worked at Norwich Cathedral.

For most parish churches in the Middle Ages there were no seats for the congregation. Benches first appeared in significant numbers in the fifteenth and sixteenth centuries, part of the great rebuilding and outpouring of popular piety in the late Middle Ages. Apart from being a status symbol, benches answered the desire for greater comfort in church in a period when sermons were increasingly preached to parish congregations. Medieval benches are variable in style, and are concentrated in a few regions. In Worcestershire the benches are generally plain; in Norfolk and Suffolk green men are notable by their rarity on bench ends in a region where there are numerous carvings of monsters. Benches with green men are concentrated in a few areas, especially Somerset, Devon and the borders of Lincolnshire, Leicestershire and Rutland. They were popular throughout the sixteenth century in various forms, spanning and outliving the Reformation. Dating of these bench ends can be difficult, but there are examples pre-dating the Reformation that follow the trend found in architectural carving.

Misericords at Richmond (North Yorkshire) were made in 1511 and include a green man with a human face, a style that harks back to the previous century.

Bench ends at Crowcombe (Somerset) include some of the most interesting green-man carvings in Britain. One bench end [right] shows a flat asymmetrically ugly mask with vine trails issuing from the mouth, and pike-like fish emerging from the ears. Others show foliage emanating from a monster's mouth [far right] and, most enigmatic of all, growing out of the sleeves of outstretched hands [below].

Bench ends at Crowcombe (Somerset) are dated 1534. They can be seen as part of the major improvements in the church that began in 1515, when the parish built a separate church house across the road to accommodate the secular functions that used to take place inside the church. This allowed the body of the church to be filled with seating. On the Crowcombe bench ends there are three conventional green men, three where the foliage is emitted from the mouths of monsters or fish and four where it emerges from the sleeves of outstretched arms. Three green men have distinctly flat faces, with asymmetrically placed eyes. In this they resemble (although they can hardly have been copied from) gorgons of Greek art. These women were so ugly that they could turn men to stone, quite a challenge for craftsmen to represent on hoplite shields. These late-medieval green men are also a studied attempt to create ugliness, and to that extent a representation of sin, a theme developed in another of the carvings where two naked men are tangled in the branches spewing from a monster's mouth. At Crowcombe these masks are distinct from the portraits and profiles of real people found on the other benches. Even if they were idealised and copied from printed sources, the Renaissance heads are convincingly human, but the green men are not. The mask spewing foliage appears regularly in sixteenth-century west-Somerset bench ends, clearly as a local preference, whereas in north Devon in the same period most of the green men are leaf masks. Their flat faces are similar to the bosses found in roofs.

The other place where medieval green men occur is on tombs. Lifelike effigies were carved in stone or engraved in brass, placed on chest tombs or in arched recesses. Skulls and cadavers symbolised death, while fashionable dress and mourning figures known as weepers signalled what these people had been on earth. Green men appear on the margins of this subject matter. They can appear as relatively inconspicuous figures on the arches that frame the tombs, like the ones at Christ Church Cathedral (Oxford), Norbury (Staffordshire) and Bredon (Worcestershire). At Harpswell (Lincolnshire) a foliate head is at the feet of the effigy of the rector, William Harrington, where a pet dog is often to be found. One can also be found on the Tomb of Christ – a type of ceremonial tomb that was fashionable in the fourteenth century – at Hawton (Nottinghamshire). Tombs are one of the few places where green men outlived the Middle Ages.

Benches at Barwick (Somerset) are dated 1533, on the eve of the Reformation, and include this green man, with already a hint of Renaissance style.

Below left: Although green-man carvings occur quite frequently on medieval tombs they are often inconspicuous. At Bredon (Worcestershire), an eroded green man links the arches above small-scale effigies of a man and wife on a grave slab dating from the early to mid-fourteenth century.

Left: This demon spouting foliage appears on the arch of a fourteenth-century tomb recess at Tewkesbury Abbey (Gloucestershire).

AFTER THE REFORMATION

TWO THINGS happened in the mid-sixteenth century that brought about a
decline in popularity of green-man carvings: the Reformation and the
Renaissance. The Renaissance was the rediscovery of classical art, but artistic
fashions have never been static, and nor were they in late-medieval Britain.
Bestiaries had been popular from the twelfth until the fourteenth centuries,
but as their popularity declined so did the moral force of their animals and
monsters. By the sixteenth century apocalyptic creatures of the kind invented
in Bruegel and Bosch paintings were more numerous in churches than
bestiary staples like the wyvern and the basilisk. The Renaissance was another,
greater force for change. It brought a new vocabulary of art into Britain,
such as nymphs and Roman gods, as well as the caryatids, putti and cherubim
that became common on funeral monuments, which is the best place to
experience the Renaissance in churches. Increasing popularity of Renaissance
decoration had the effect of rendering the medieval iconography old-
fashioned.

The second, more decisive factor was the religious Reformation. It began
in earnest with the break with Rome in 1534, gathered pace with the closure
of monasteries between 1536 and 1539, and led to wholesale changes to
religious practices during the reign of Edward VI (1547–53). After briefly
reverting to Catholicism, a national Protestant church was established
following Elizabeth's accession in 1558. Protestants were suspicious of
imagery in churches. At worst, they saw pictures of saints as objects of
idolatry, and people who prayed for saints to intercede on their behalf were
treating that saint as if it were a deity, in a religion where there is only one
God. Although this did not affect green men specifically, green men existed
at the margins of a visual religious culture, and when the core of the culture
collapsed the margins followed suit, albeit more slowly.

The early sixteenth century had been a period when parish churches
were still being enlarged and rebuilt, but by the 1550s taxation and liturgical
changes challenged the resources and enthusiasm for new church building.
One reason that architectural green men declined was that there was a sharp

Opposite:
This Renaissance
wall monument at
Bosbury
(Herefordshire)
was erected in
1578 in memory of
Richard Harford. It
incorporates crude
classical caryatids
(figures acting as
columns) but also
incongruous green
men.

In Bristol St Mary Redcliffe is the monument to the Reverend Richard Sandford (d. 1721) by James Paty the Elder, one of a prominent local family of masons, carvers and architects. In the lower panel, or apron, is a skull issuing branches, one of the last 'medieval' green men.

Bench ends at Spaxton (Somerset) are dated 1561. The face of a green man occupies only a small part of the carving and appears secondary to the flowers.

decline in building. Although some new churches continued to be built in the Gothic style into the seventeenth century, the taste for lavish decoration had passed. A direct impact on the number of green-man carvings was also caused by changes in liturgical practices that rendered certain fixtures redundant. When monasteries were disbanded there was no longer any need for misericords because there were no longer monks or canons observing the Catholic liturgy. Likewise churches no longer needed rood screens, many of which were removed in the name of de-mystifying the sacraments. Monuments and heraldry continued to be a focus of symbolic imagery. As an art form, funeral monuments flourished in the seventeenth and eighteenth centuries and occasionally death was represented by mixing foliage and skulls, although the principal images associated with death were urns, skulls and flaming torches.

One place where green men continued to thrive in the Reformation years was on the ends of benches in parish churches. Most parishes had no or very little seating before the Reformation, and even by the end of the century benches were probably found in only a significant minority of parish churches. In Somerset and Devon green-man bench ends remained popular after the Reformation. However, there is a shift from the moralistic overtones of pre-Reformation benches to the ornamental schemes that followed it. In many cases, therefore, greenery sprouts from the mouth of a facial mask in the same manner that it grows out of a vase.

Leaf masks are found in various forms of classical architecture or applied art from the sixteenth to the eighteenth century. Most of it is found on or in secular buildings rather than churches, in a period when it was a decorative device. For example, the great French ironsmith Jean Tijou, who

Sixteenth-century bench ends at Churchstanton (Somerset), re-used as the front for a gallery in 1830, are Renaissance in character and include this decorative rather than moral green man.

introduced Baroque wrought-ironwork to Britain in the 1690s, incorporated leaf masks in the privy garden screens at Hampton Court, and for a screen at St Paul's Cathedral, which shares the same decorative vocabulary. One of his followers, William Edney, also used leaf masks for his screen at Bristol St Mary Redcliffe, and for the gateway outside Tewkesbury Abbey where a fish disgorges foliage (an image with a medieval precedent).

High Bickington (Devon) bench ends belong to the second half of the sixteenth century and are a curious cross-breeding of medieval and Renaissance styles. Here classical putti are made to grow stems from their mouths.

Tiverton church (Devon) was largely rebuilt in 1853–6 by Edward Ashworth, architect of Exeter. The demon on this capital is probably a faithful reproduction from the medieval work that was replaced.

A revival of Gothic architecture started in the eighteenth century, but flourished from the mid-nineteenth century. It was inspired by a renewed interest in all things medieval, from its religious practices to its architecture, and was pioneered by architects such as A.W.N. Pugin who wanted to build in an authentic medieval style. The nation's stock of medieval churches was also in poor condition by the early nineteenth century, which resulted in a wave of restoration and improvement. Many surviving architectural green men are the product of nineteenth-century restoration. With new buildings came a fresh delight in ornamentation. Grotesques and gargoyles abound on

Evesham All Saints (Worcestershire) was restored by local architect Frederick Preedy in the 1870s. The south-aisle roof has painted bosses, including this green man with foliage issuing from mouth and eyes, which may faithfully reproduce the medieval boss it replaced.

Hallaton (Leicestershire) church was restored in 1889 by Charles Kirk of Sleaford. He rebuilt all the roofs, which include mostly foliage bosses, except for two green-man bosses in the south aisle. The roofs may have been modelled on the previous roofs.

Cockermouth All Saints (Cumbria) was built in 1852 by London architect Joseph Clarke. Alternate piers in the nave have capitals with demon or human heads biting foliage trails.

Birstall church (West Yorkshire) was largely rebuilt in the 1860s by the Leeds architect W. H. Crossland. His taste for lavish decoration, and use of abundant foliage carving, is well represented at Birstall where one of the capitals shows the foliage issuing from feline heads.

the exterior of Victorian buildings, where green men also started to appear. They are also found in many of the contexts in which they had appeared in medieval buildings, particularly on roof bosses and the capitals of arches. Their inclusion was one, albeit minor, touchstone of authentic medieval style. Although Victorian scholars studied and unearthed evidence of medieval religious practices, and amassed a vast knowledge of the vocabulary of Gothic architecture, they did not provide an explanation for the green man and why he was so common in medieval churches. Writers such as John Ruskin and William Morris, who were passionate about medieval architecture and nature, do not mention him. Victorian green men are decorative features that have lost their moral force.

The organisation and creative process of architecture had changed since the medieval period. Architects often now took responsibility for the design of all aspects of a building, including its furnishing. Architects also controlled the design of the gargoyles and bosses, taking away any inventive freedom enjoyed by medieval freemasons. Sir George Gilbert Scott (1811–78) incorporated green men into some of his buildings, as did the many pupils of his that went on to become successful architects in their own right.

Church furnishing was undertaken by specialist firms who produced their own designs if they were not receiving instructions from an architect. Some misericords were made for Victorian churches, usually as a result of careful research – Sir George Gilbert Scott, for example, copied designs from New College, Oxford, in the reinstatement of misericords at Canterbury Cathedral. Even so, nineteenth-century green-man carvings have a vitality that makes them unmistakably Victorian. The best examples are the choir stalls at Lancing College chapel, designed by Sir George Gilbert Scott and Walter Tower, and the misericords at Wintringham (North Yorkshire) designed in 1889 by Temple Moore (1856–1920), an accomplished architect of the late Gothic revival and a devout Anglo-Catholic. Nineteenth-century

church benches are not noted for their artistic enterprise and green men are rarely found on them, with exceptions like the set at Northington (Hampshire) by Sir T. G. Jackson (1835–1924). Jackson had been a pupil of Scott, one of whose sons, George Gilbert Scott Junior (1839–97), himself designed green-man misericords for Bakewell (Derbyshire).

Leighton church (Powys) was built by the Liverpool architect W. H. Gee, and incorporates this very un-medieval green man above the vestry doorway.

Moseley (Birmingham) church was rebuilt in 1910 by local architect P. B. Chatwin in his favoured Decorated style, and includes well-preserved green men on the eaves.

Right: Choir stalls at Tideswell (Derbyshire) were made in the 1870s and convincing medieval features include misericords and small roundels with green men.

Below: The choir stalls at Wintringham (North Yorkshire) were designed by Temple Lushington Moore and carved in 1889 by James Elwell. It is difficult to imagine how its green-man carvings could have been taken to represent sin and mortality. The green man had become part of an antiquarian repertoire.

Green men declined from the end of the nineteenth century as the architecture that sustained them fell out of fashion. In any case, architects had started incorporating green-man carvings in secular as well as religious buildings, a sure sign that it was a decorative rather than a moral image. The Modern movement in architecture had had enough of lavish decoration,

Misericords at Bakewell were designed by George Gilbert Scott Junior and are a studied attempt to recreate authentic medieval stalls, which inevitably meant that one of the misericords is a green man.

and its clean lines and bold detail were not conducive to decoration. In the rediscovery of the green man in the twentieth century, from Lady Raglan to the artist John Piper, the image moved beyond the church into the secular world and, eventually, to a new set of meanings.

Green men appeared on many secular buildings from the latter half of the nineteenth century, as illustrated here on James Miller's St Enoch subway station, Glasgow, built in 1896.

FURTHER READING

There are many books about green men but not all of them use historical methods or, in fact, claim to be history in the conventional sense. Books that best discuss the origins, and the medieval and modern meanings of green men, are listed below.

Basford, Kathleen. *The Green Man*. D.S. Brewer, 1978.
Doel, Fran and Geoff. *The Green Man in Britain*. Tempus, 2000.
MacDermott, Mercia. *Explore Green Men*. Explore Books, second edition 2006.
Weir, Anthony and James Jerman. *Images of Lust: Sexual carvings on medieval churches*. Batsford, 1986.

PLACES TO VISIT

Green-man carvings can be found in a large number of churches, but only a selection is mentioned here. Unfortunately green-man carvings are rarely mentioned in the *Buildings of England* series of architectural guides, being usually only of marginal interest. Green men are often found in obscure and poorly lit parts of churches, or are unobtrusive, and are therefore difficult to see and easy to miss. Perseverance is recommended, and it should be remembered that in the list below the churches have other features of note that make them worth visiting. In the lists below carvings are interior features unless otherwise stated.

ENGLAND

Bedfordshire
  Studham (font).
Berkshire
  Langley Marsh (arcade label stops). Padworth (chancel arch).
Buckinghamshire
  Leckhampstead (font). Monks Risborough (corbels).
Cambridgeshire
  Balsham (misericord). Cambridge, King's College Chapel (roofs, chapel screen, misericord). Castor (chancel arch). Ely Cathedral (Lady Chapel roof, misericords). Landbeach (roof). Over (misericords).
  Peterborough, St John the Baptist (porch roof). Tydd St Giles (font).
Cheshire
  Chester Cathedral (misericord). Nantwich (stained glass in north transept, porch roof).

Cornwall

Lanreath (screen). Lanteglos-by-Fowey (bench ends). Lostwithiel (font).

Cumbria

Bridekirk (font). Carlisle Cathedral (capitals, corbels). Cartmel Priory (misericords). Cockermouth, All Saints (capitals). Crosthwaite (font). Gosforth (chancel arch). Lowther (capitals).

Derbyshire

Bakewell (misericords). Tideswell (choir stalls).

Devon

Chagford (roof). Down St Mary (bench end). Exeter Cathedral (misericords, roofs). High Bickington (bench ends). Kings Nympton (corbels). Luppitt (font, roof). Marwood (rood screen). Newton St Cyres (roof). North Bovey (corbels). Nymet Rowland (roof). Nymet Tracey (roof). Ottery St Mary (corbels, capitals). Sampford Courtenay (roofs). South Molton (capitals). South Tawton (roofs). Spreyton (roof). Tiverton (capitals). Ugborough (corbels). Widecombe-in-the-Moor (corbels). Woodbury (capitals).

A cadaverous head grows leaves from its mouth and eye sockets on a roof boss at Sampford Courtenay (Devon).

Dorset

Dorchester St Peter (roof). Sherborne Abbey (misericord). Upwey (capital).

Durham

Durham Cathedral (cloister roof).

Essex

Belchamp (misericord). Mount Nessing (capital).

Gloucestershire and Bristol

Avening (chancel roof). Bristol: Cathedral (misericords); St Mark (bench ends); St Mary Redcliffe (stained glass, corbels, bosses, eighteenth-century monument, iron screen). Dumbleton (doorway). Elkstone (doorway). North Nibley (capital). Quenington (doorway). Tewkesbury Abbey (roofs).

Hampshire

Northington (window tracery, doorway, label stops, bench ends). Winchester: Cathedral (choir stalls, misericords, porch roof); St Cross (aisle roof).

Herefordshire

Garway (tower arch). Hereford: All Saints (misericords); Cathedral (aisle roofs). Kilpeck (doorway, west window). Leominster Priory (doorway). Much Marcle (capitals). Rock (doorway). Rowlstone (doorway).

Hertfordshire
Stevenage St Nicholas and Holy Trinity (misericord).
Kent
Canterbury Cathedral (cloister roof). Minster-in-Thanet (misericord). Rochester Cathedral (roof). Wade St Nicholas (capitals, roofs). Wingham (misericord).
Lancashire
Whalley (choir stalls, misericords). Wigan All Saints (external carvings).
Leicestershire
Buckminster (corbels). Croxton Kerriel (bench end). Frisby-on-the-Wreake (nave roof, choir stalls). Harston (roof corbels). Horninghold (doorway). Little Dalby (capitals). Lutterworth (roof). Ryhall (corbel table). Sileby (roof). Sproxton (roofs). Thurcaston (tower arch).
Lincolnshire
Barkston (screen). Boston (south doorway). Brant Broughton (porch and nave roofs). Cadney (corbel). Claypole (capitals, corbels). Crowland Abbey (roof). Grantham St Wulfram (eaves). Harpswell (monument). Lincoln Cathedral (cloister roof, misericords). Pinchbeck (corbel). Silk Willoughby (bench back). Stow (font). Temple Bruer (capitals).
London
Temple church (capitals). St Katharine, Butcher Row (misericord). St Paul's Cathedral (aisle screens). Westminster Abbey, Henry VII's chapel (misericords).
Norfolk
King's Lynn St Margaret (misericord). Norwich: Cathedral (misericords, cloister roof); St Ethelbert's Gatehouse (vault); St Stephen (misericord). Salle (roof). Weston Longville (chancel walls). Wilton (chancel screen).
Northamptonshire
Benefield (vestry corbel). Finedon (capitals). Great Doddington

Misericords at Norwich Cathedral were carved in the early fifteenth century, and include two fine examples of green men.

One misericord at Higham Ferrers (Northamptonshire), carved in the 1420s, shows a stylised lion's head growing leaves from the corners of its mouth.

(misericord). Higham Ferrers (misericord). Northampton St Peter (capitals, grave slab). Wadenhoe (corbel). Wakerley (chancel arch).

Northumberland

Embleton (porch roof). Hexham Abbey (misericords).

Nottinghamshire

Newark (capitals, misericord). Southwell Minster (chapter house, misericord).

Oxfordshire

Adderbury (misericords). Aston Tirrold (chancel arch). Burford (capital). Charney Bassett (doorway). Dorchester Abbey (corbel). Fullbrook (nave roof). Fritwell (doorway). Oxford: Christ Church Cathedral (choir stalls, thirteenth- and seventeenth-century tombs); New College Chapel (misericords). South Moreton (label stop). Sparsholt (monument). Standlake (roof). Stanton Harcourt (tomb).

Rutland

Clipsham (bench ends). Ketton (bench end). Oakham (capital). Tinwell (doorway).

Shropshire

Battlefield (corbel). Eaton-under-Heywood (roof). Linley (doorway, font). Ludlow (misericords). Morville (font). Stottesdon (font). Tong (misericords).

Somerset

Barwick (bench end). Batcombe (doorway).

This classic head with hawthorn mask is on one of the labels stops – the carvings at the ends of the hood moulds over arches and windows – in the Southwell Minster chapter house.

Bicknoller (bench end). Bishops Lydeard (bench ends). Cheddar (bench ends). Churchstanton (gallery). Cothelstone (bench ends). Crowcombe (bench ends). Culbone (roof). Glastonbury St John (transept roof). Halse (roundel, capitals). Lullington (font, tower arch). Nailsea (capital). Queen Camel (roof boss). Spaxton (bench ends). Stogursey (bench end). Wells: Cathedral (nave, chapter house); St Cuthbert (porch roof).

Staffordshire

Cannock St Luke (eaves). Lichfield Cathedral (aisle roofs).

Suffolk

Cotton (porch capital). Dennington (capital). Earl Stonham (roof).

Sussex, East

Winchelsea (monument).

Sussex, West

Boxgrove Priory (de la Warre chapel roof). Chichester Cathedral (aisle roofs). Lancing College Chapel (choir stalls).

Warwickshire and Birmingham

Barcheston (corbel). Coventry Holy Trinity (misericord). Moseley (eaves). Stratford-upon-Avon (misericord).

Wiltshire

Amesbury (roof). Bowden Hill (external corbels). Chiseldon (eaves, roof). Ludgershall (corbels). Mere (misericord). Salisbury: Cathedral (misericords); St Thomas (misericord). Stanton St Quintin (roof). Sutton Benger (capital).

Worcestershire

Holt (doorway, font). Overbury (bench end). Pershore Abbey (chancel vault). Strensham (screen). Worcester Cathedral (choir stalls, cloister roof).

This gaunt and hairless head on a misericord at Stratford-upon-Avon (Warwickshire) serves to link death with greenery, a reminder that all flesh is grass. The supporters have small heads at the centre of the flowers.

Yorkshire, East

Beverley: Minster (misericord, capital); St Mary (external capitals, misericords). Swine (misericord).

Yorkshire, North

Barton-le-Street (doorway). Bolton Abbey (nave roof). Coxwold (roof). Fountains Abbey (window in Chapel of the Nine Altars). Liverton (chancel arch). Old Malton (misericord). Patrick Brompton (stained glass fragment). Riccall (doorway). Richmond (misericord, porch roof). Ripon Cathedral (misericord, corbel). Wintringham (choir stalls, misericords). York Minster (corbels, roofs, especially chapter house).

Yorkshire, South

Loversall (misericord). Sheffield Cathedral (Lady Chapel roof). Silkstone (roof).

Yorkshire, West

Halifax St John (misericord).

SCOTLAND

Dumfries and Galloway

Glenluce Abbey (chapter house roof).

Midlothian

Rosslyn Chapel (roof).

Perthshire

Dunblane Cathedral (misericord).

WALES

Monmouthshire and Newport

Llangwm Uchaf (crossing arches). Llantilio Crosseny (crossing arches). Newport St Woolos Cathedral (font).

Pembrokeshire

Haverfordwest (roofs). St David's Cathedral (misericord).

Powys

Brecon Cathedral (font). Leighton (vestry doorway). Llananno (rood screen). Llanbadarn Fawr (doorway). Pennant Melangell (rood screen).

INDEX

Page numbers in italics refer to
illustrations